Ma...er

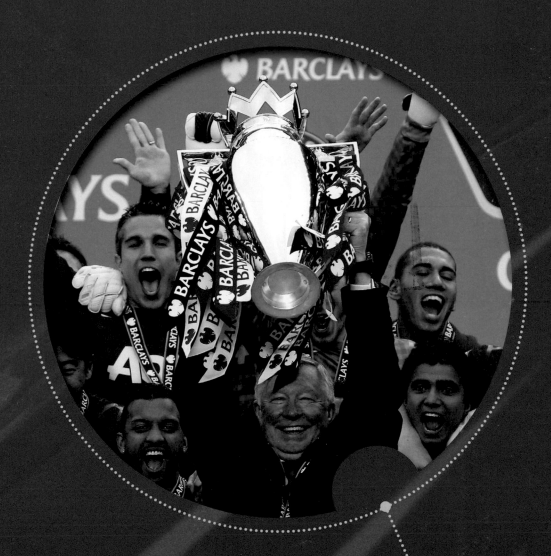

Adam Sutherland

Updated and published in paperback in 2016 by Wayland
Copyright © Wayland 2016

Wayland
An imprint of
Hachette Children's Group
Part of Hodder & Stoughton
Carmelite House
50 Victoria Embankment
London EC4Y 0DZ

Commissioning editor: Annabel Stones
Designer: LittleRedAnt (Anthony Hannant)
Picture researcher: Shelley Noronha

ISBN: 978 0 7502 8945 0
Library e-book ISBN 978 0 7502 8541 4

Dewey categorisation: 338.7'61-dc23

Printed in China

MIX
Paper from
responsible sources
FSC
www.fsc.org   FSC® C104740

10 9 8 7 6 5 4 3 2 1

Wayland is a division of Hachette Children's Group, an Hachette UK company.
www.hachette.co.uk

Picture acknowledgements: The author and publisher would like to thank the following for
allowing their pictures to be reproduced in this publication: Cover: Richard Klune/Corbis; p.4, left:
Shutterstock; p. 4, right: Shutterstock; p.5: AFP/Getty Images; p.6: Popperfoto/Getty Images; p.7:
Colorsport/Corbis; p.8: Mary Evans/Pharcide; p.9: Colorsport/Corbis; p.10: Popperfoto/Getty Images;
p.11, top: Colorsport/REX; p. 11, bottom: Shutterstock; p.12: Getty Images; p.13: Bob Thomas/Getty
Images; p.14: Colorsport/REX; p.15 & title page: Getty Images; p.16: Photoshot; p.17: Shutterstock;
p.18: Getty Images; p.19: Photoshot; p.20: Fotosports/Photoshot; p.21: Man Utd via Getty Images;
p.22, left: Shutterstock; p.22, right: Bob Thomas/Getty Images; p. 23 & p. 31: Shutterstock; p.24 & 32:
Shutterstock; p.25: Shutterstock; p.26, all images: Shutterstock; p.27: Man Utd via Getty Images.

Contents

All change at the top

It's May 2013, and Manchester United reign supreme. They have just won a record 20th League title by 11 points from rivals Manchester City whilst earlier in the year, they became the first team in the world to be valued at $3 billion (£1.8 bn). Could things get any better?

The world of sport, like the world of business, is all about change. Manchester United's manager of 26 years, Sir Alex Ferguson, retired at the end of the season. He brought the club a staggering 38 trophies and helped build one of the most valuable brands in sport.

Successors David Moyes and Louis Van Gaal failed to match Ferguson's success with league finishes dropping to fourth, seventh and fifth, meaning United missed out on lucrative UEFA Champions League football.

In May 2016, Jose Mourinho was appointed as the new manager of the club. Can he bring success on the pitch for Manchester United and how will the business continue to cope and prosper without Sir Alex?

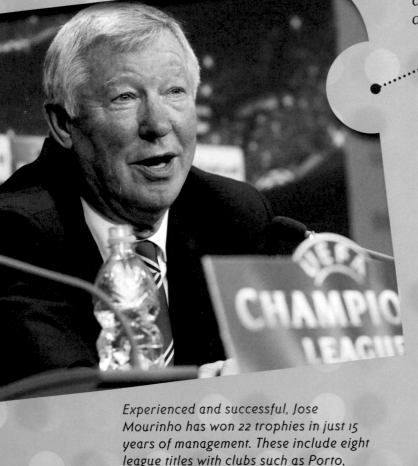

Sir Alex Ferguson retired as manager of Manchester United after bringing exceptional levels of success to the club.

Experienced and successful, Jose Mourinho has won 22 trophies in just 15 years of management. These include eight league titles with clubs such as Porto, Inter Milan, Chelsea and Real Madrid.

Manchester United by numbers*

62 trophies won

69.6m Facebook connections

200 licensees in 130 countries

2.2bn worldwide TV viewers for games in 2014–15

$559m (£347m) seven-year sponsorship deal with General Motors (beginning with the 2014–15 season)

2m replica shirts sold per year

110m official supporters in China

* All figures correct at the time of writing

> "We don't give in, we play right to the end... It's part of the make-up of the team. This team doesn't understand the word defeat."
>
> *Sir Alex Ferguson, Alex Ferguson: My Autobiography, 2013*

Manchester United's success on the field has been mirrored by its growth. Its 75,766-capacity stadium, known as the 'Theatre of Dreams', has averaged over 99 per cent attendance for the last 15 years, with a total attendance for home league games in the 2014–15 season of almost 1.4 billion – an average of 72,991 per game.

Today the club is a truly global sporting brand, with 659 million followers worldwide. Its website, www.manutd.com, is published in seven languages and regularly attracts over 43 million page views per month. Over five million items bearing the club's name and logo are sold every year – including two million replica shirts.

This book tells the story of the rise of Manchester United from a small football club to an international business. It looks at the key people who shaped the brand, the highs and lows, and what lies ahead for the one of the most successful and valuable sports clubs in history.

Manchester United official merchandise in a store in New Delhi, India. The club's signing of Asian players has helped its fanbase to grow.

Humble beginnings

Manchester United began life in 1878 as Newton Heath LYR Football Club. It was formed by the Carriage and Wagon department of the Lancashire and Yorkshire Railway depot in the Manchester district that bore its name.

The railway company funded the team and paid the lease on its first home ground – a field close to the railway yard. Organised football leagues were in their infancy, but nevertheless, in the 1882–83 season the team played 26 friendly matches. By 1886 it was signing players with a national reputation, including club captain Jack Powell, and brothers Jack and Roger Doughty.

In 1890, after being refused admission to the newly formed Football League, Newton Heath and 11 other clubs formed the Football Alliance. In 1892, the Alliance merged with the Football League and Newton Heath was elected to the First Division.

By this time they had dropped LYR from their name, although most players were still railway employees. The club had also become a limited company, issuing 2,000 shares at £1 each, and had moved to a new ground in Bank Street, Clayton.

Unfortunately, success on the pitch did not follow the ambitious plans. In 1893–94 Newton Heath was the first team to be relegated to the Second Division, and in January 1902, with debts of £2,670 (equivalent to £200,000 today) the club was served with a winding-up order. Fortunately, club captain Harry Stafford and three local businessmen each agreed to invest £500 to save the club. In April 1902, in honour of its fresh start, the club changed its named to Manchester United and team colours became red shirts and white shorts.

An illustration from 1892 shows Newton Heath in action wearing green and yellow shirts.

Forming a company

A 'limited' or 'incorporated' company is a business owned by shareholders (people who own shares in the company), and run by directors. The company's shares have a basic value, for example £1 each, which stays the same. They also have a 'market value', which goes up and down depending on how good an investment the shares are judged to be by people outside the company who want to buy those shares.

The newly named Manchester United (in trademark red shirts) won the League in 1907–08.

Brains

Behind The Brand

John Henry Davies
Former owner of Manchester United FC

Davies was a wealthy brewery owner who formed a consortium to buy Newton Heath in 1902 and wiped out its debts. Legend has it that Davies started talking to club captain Harry Stafford when Stafford's dog approached him at a fundraising event for the club.

Davies was an important figure in the club's early development – not only changing the club's name and team colours, but also expanding the size of the ground and overseeing the appointment of the first manager, and the purchase of new players who helped Manchester United return to the First Division.

Fighting with debt

In 1903, Manchester United employed its first real team manager, Ernest Mangnall. The goal was to win promotion back to the First Division, where bigger crowds would mean greater match-day income.

In 1905, Manchester City were hit by a scandal when the club was accused of taking bribes to lose their final game of the season. Seventeen players were banned from playing for the club ever again, and the Football Association forced City to auction off their players at the Queen's Hotel in Manchester.

Mangnall signed a number of the disgraced City players, including winger Billy Meredith. Meredith was regarded as the best player in England at the time; Mangnall signed him for £500. With a much-strengthened team, Manchester United won promotion back to the First Division in 1906. They quickly established themselves back in the top flight, winning their first League Championship in 1908, the FA Cup in 1909, and a second League title in 1911.

At the end of the 1911-12 season, however, Mangnall crossed town to manage Manchester City, and was replaced by John Bentley. Before his departure, in 1910, Mangnall had been largely responsible for moving the club from Clayton to their current home of Old Trafford. Although the new ground was a great step forward, the Football League was suspended at the outbreak of the First World War, meaning the club was still responsible for the running costs of Old Trafford with no money coming in.

An aerial view of Old Trafford from 1922. The club moved to the ground in 1910.

FOOTBALL GROUND
OLD TRAFFORD
FROM AN
AEROPLANE

RESERVE MATCH
IN PROGRESS

The 1920s and 1930s were a period of relegation and promotion, with added turmoil off the pitch. On Christmas Eve 1931 there was no money to pay the players' wages, and Manchester United were close to going out of business. Local businessman James W. Gibson invested £30,000 in the club, and appointed a new manager, Scott Duncan. The team's successes on the field, including promotion to the First Division, led to increased attendances, but money remained scarce, and by the outbreak of the Second World War the club were £70,000 in debt. Could they survive?

Brains

Behind The Brand

Ernest Mangnall
First manager of Manchester United

Former goalkeeper Mangnall managed Manchester United from 1903 to 1912 and remains the third most successful manager in the club's history, behind Sir Alex Ferguson and Sir Matt Busby.

Mangnall's team won the First Division title twice, as well as one FA Cup and two FA Charity Shields. He then managed Manchester City from 1912 until 1924 – the only manager to date who has managed both clubs.

Ernest Mangnall joined Manchester United in 1903 and led the club to the first ever League title in the 1907–08 season.

Business Matters

Profit and loss

A profit and loss statement is a company's financial report that indicates how the revenue (money received from the sale of products and services before expenses are taken out) is transformed into the net income (the result after all revenues and expenses have been accounted for). It shows the revenues for a specific period, and the cost and expenses charged against those revenues. The purpose of the profit and loss statement is to show company managers and investors whether the company made or lost money during the period being reported.

The Busby Babes

World War Two further added to the club's troubles. Old Trafford was damaged in German bombing raids. While rebuilding was taking place – thanks to a grant of over £20,000 from the War Damage Commission – home games were played at Manchester City's ground. This cost Manchester United £5,000 per year plus a percentage of all tickets sold.

Manchester United were long overdue some success on the field. In October 1945 the club appointed Matt Busby as manager. Busby's hands-on approach to team selection, player transfers and even the organization of training sessions, soon paid off. He led the team to second-place finishes in the League in 1947, 1948 and 1949, and to FA Cup victory in 1948 – the club's first major trophy for 37 years. In 1952, the club won the First Division, its first League title for 41 years.

Mindful of Manchester United's financial limitations, Busby began selling some of the club's older players, and replacing them with youngsters from the reserve team. By the end of 1951, the team became known as the 'Busby Babes' and by the 1955–56 season, Busby's youngsters won the League by an 11-point margin with a team average age of just 22. Much credit has to be given to Busby's network of football scouts, who unearthed talent across the north of England and into Ireland and Northern Ireland.

“ I never wanted Manchester United to be second to anybody. Only the best would be good enough. ”

Sir Matt Busby, taken from a profile in The Telegraph, 2008

The 'Busby Babes': Manchester United's title-winning team from 1955–56 and 1956–57.

A 1958 newspaper report of the Manchester United team's air crash disaster.

However, disaster struck Busby's team on the way home from a European Cup match in February 1958. The plane carrying Manchester United players, officials and journalists crashed near Munich, Germany, killing 23 people, including eight players, and injuring several more. Busby himself was seriously hurt in the crash.

Busby rebuilt his team throughout the 1960s, mixing established names, such as Denis Law and Bobby Charlton, with young talent, such as George Best (the 1960s equivalent of David Beckham). They won the FA Cup in 1963, and the League in 1965 and 1967.

In 1968, Manchester United became the first English club to win the European Cup, beating Benfica of Portugal 4–1 in the final. Significantly, Busby's cup-winning side only contained two players that the club had bought – the rest were free transfers or had come through the United youth ranks.

Brains

Behind The Brand

Sir Matt Busby
Former Manchester United manager

Busby joined Manchester United straight from the army, and brought discipline and style to his team's performances. He also introduced a sense of branding that brought international awareness to the club. For example, Busby adopted the name 'The Red Devils' for the club. The club began incorporating the devil logo into match programmes and scarves, and in 1970 the club badge was redesigned, with a devil in the centre holding a pitchfork.

The statue of the legendary Sir Matt Busby was erected outside Old Trafford in 1996.

Life after Busby

In any business, following in the footsteps of a successful manager is never easy. From 1969 to 1986 Manchester United hired and fired five managers trying to find a suitable successor to Sir Matt Busby.

Many companies attempt to recruit from within, for example Tim Cook becoming Apple CEO after Steve Jobs' death. To try and ensure continuity at the club, Busby's immediate successor was reserve team coach and former United player Wilf McGuinness. Unfortunately, McGuinness struggled under the weight of expectation. After one season, Busby returned temporarily, and successfully pulled the team clear of relegation.

Manchester United manager Ron Atkinson talks to his players before extra time in the 1983 FA Cup Final.

Frank O'Farrell was the next name in charge. He was an appointment from outside the club, having successfully helped Leicester City win promotion to the First Division. The team finished eighth in the League in his one full season. However, his team began the next season without a win in nine games, and in December 1972 he was replaced by Scotland manager Tommy Docherty.

Although a Scot, like Busby, Docherty was another outsider to the club. Nevertheless, he strengthened the team with a series of signings, but saw the club relegated in 1974.

Continuity

All businesses need to keep trading and functioning after the departure of a CEO or, in the case of a football club, a manager. This is done in three ways.

Resilience: important business functions — from training to the selling of match-day tickets — are designed to be unaffected by most disruptions.

Contingency: often a deputy, for example a first team coach, is put in charge of the team while a new manager is found; they often then go on to assist a new manager with inside knowledge.

Recovery: a new manager is hired to hopefully raise team performance to higher levels.

Like Busby, Docherty then started to build a team around young players, and United were promoted at the first attempt. They reached the FA Cup Final in 1976, losing to Southampton, but lifted the trophy the following year.

Docherty was replaced by former Chelsea manager Dave Sexton in the summer of 1977. Sexton's track record was strong – he had won the FA Cup and UEFA Cup Winners' Cup with Chelsea, but he was unable to repeat that success in Manchester. He departed at the end of the 1980–81 season to be replaced by West Bromwich Albion manager Ron Atkinson.

Atkinson signed midfielder Bryan Robson from his former club, who became one of the club's all-time greats. Atkinson won the FA Cup in 1983 and 1985, but was sacked in 1986 with the club close to the relegation zone. Manchester United's most successful period in history was about to begin.

Brains

Behind The Brand

Louis Edwards
Former chairman of Manchester United

Manchester businessman Edwards was an investor in the club from the late 1950s, and by 1965 owned over 50 per cent of the club's shares. He was club chairman from 1965 to his death in 1980, overseeing First Division, FA Cup and European Cup victories. With Edwards' help, the club developed the United Road Stand at a cost of £350,000, incorporating British football's first executive boxes.

Louis Edwards was a Manchester United fan who joined the board the day after the Munich air disaster in 1958.

Alex Ferguson becomes manager

In 1986, Alex Ferguson joined the club from Aberdeen. The new manager was a virtual unknown in England, but went on to eclipse the achievements of all his Manchester United predecessors.

Great achievements require teamwork, but also great management. This fact is as true when talking about the development of the smartphone, as the transformation of Manchester United into the most successful UK club of the last 20 years.

Ferguson joined the club in November 1986 and started slowly. The team finished 11th in two of his first three seasons, but developments were taking place – new talent was being

signed, and Ferguson was rebuilding the club's youth system to unearth great homegrown young players.

In 1990, the team won the FA Cup, and in 1993 secured its first League title since 1967. Success brings clubs greater prize money, but also benefits such as a larger fanbase and an increase in merchendise sales.

Manchester United manager Sir Alex Ferguson leads his team onto the pitch for the 1990 FA Cup Final.

Sir Alex Ferguson's trophy cabinet

- Premier League – 13
- UEFA Champions League – 2
- FA Cup – 5
- League Cup – 4
- UEFA Cup Winner's Cup – 1
- UEFA Super Cup – 1
- FIFA Club World Cup – 1
- Intercontinental Cup – 1
- FA Community Shield – 10

The following year – and for the first time since 1957 – United won a consecutive title, as well as the FA Cup. It was the first 'double' in the club's history.

In 1999, the team won an unprecedented 'treble' of Premier League, FA Cup and UEFA Champions League.

In 2009, the team equaled Liverpool's record of 18 League titles – a record they have since surpassed with a 20th League victory in the summer of 2013. The record of United's success undoubtedly helped the club's fanbase to grow internationally, as well as in the UK.

During Ferguson's 26 years in charge of the club, Manchester United won 13 Premier League titles, five FA Cups, four League Cups and two Champions Leagues. The team's success on the field, coupled with astute business partnerships, have helped establish Manchester United as a brand whose name is known around the world.

Sir Alex Ferguson lifts his final trophy for the club – the 2013 Premier League title.

Brains

Behind The Brand

Martin Edwards
Former chairman of Manchester United

Edwards became chairman in 1980, following the death of his father Louis Edwards, and remained in the role until 2002. Edwards was one of the four club directors who targeted Alex Ferguson for the manager's role, and regularly backed Ferguson in the transfer market with club-record signings (see pages 22–23). Edwards now holds the position of honorary life president of the club.

The Premiership years

In 1992, English football changed more dramatically than at any time in its 100-year history. This was due to 22 First Division clubs, including Manchester United, Arsenal and Chelsea, breaking away from the Football League to form the FA Premier League.

The new Premier League teams profited from a lucrative five-year £305-million deal with BSkyB to televise Premier League matches. Today, this deal is worth over £5.1 billion with rights shared between Sky and British Telecom (BT) to televise 168 Premier League games per season.

Each Premier League club receives a share of domestic and overseas TV rights, with additional prize money based on their League position at the end of the season. In the 2015–16 season, Manchester United received a staggering £96m. Over £19.87m was prize money for finishing fifth in the league whilst the remainder was television rights payments for their 26 live match appearances on TV and included £29.4m for overseas TV rights. In contrast, the bottom-placed team, Aston Villa, received £66m.

The dominance on the pitch for Manchester United over the 21 years of the Premier League has brought huge financial benefits to the club, and a massive worldwide fanbase. It is important to note, however, that English Premier League clubs negotiate TV rights as a group, rather than individually.

The Premier League has also become the most watched football League in the world, broadcast in 212 countries to 643 million homes with a potential audience of 4.7 billion people.

Club chairman Martin Edwards (centre) launches Manchester United's own TV channel, MUTV, with executives from Granada and BSkyB.

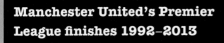
🏆 1st

2013		
2011		
2009		
2008		
2007		
2003		
2001		
2000		
1999		
1997		
1996		
1994		
1993		

🏆 2nd

2012
2010
2006
1998
1995

🏆 3rd

2005
2004
2002

Brains

Behind The Brand

Peter Kenyon
Former chief executive

Kenyon joined the Manchester United Board of Directors in 1997, and was promoted to chief executive in August 2000. He played an important role in persuading Sir Alex Ferguson to reverse his decision to retire in 2002 (Ferguson remained at the club for a further 11 years). During Kenyon's time as chief executive, Manchester United enjoyed a period of financial stability, while still twice breaking the club's transfer record for players Rio Ferdinand and Juan Sebastián Verón.

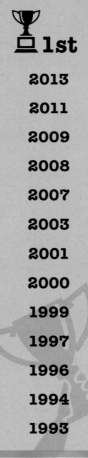

Rio Ferdinand leaves the field after a friendly in Bangkok, Thailand in July 2013. The club is now truly a global brand.

Who owns Manchester United?

Like many businesses, football clubs change ownership through their lifetime as owners retire or sell up, and new buyers enter the market. In 2005, Manchester United was sold to new American owners, the Glazers. Here's the story of the biggest purchase in English football.

The chairman of a football club is usually the person with complete or majority ownership of the club. They may be a successful business person in their own right, but they don't necessarily have any in-depth knowledge of football. The ideal chairman has a vision for the club's long-term success off the field, and employs a manager to handle transfer dealings and team tactics on the field.

During chairman Martin Edwards' time as owner of the club, Manchester United was the subject of several takeover bids. This usually happens when a potential buyer believes a business – in this case, a football club – is 'undervalued', in other words it can be bought for less than the buyer thinks it is worth. This assumption is based on a buyer's estimate of possible income – from match day ticket sales, merchandise, TV rights and so on.

Manchester United supporters protest the Glazers' ownership of the club.

Malcom Glazer's son, Avram, at the New York Stock Exchange in 2012.

There were two failed take-over bids – one in 1989 and one in 1998. Then, in 2003, American family the Glazers started to buy shares in Manchester United. They started small, with a first purchase of 2.9 per cent of shares, costing £9m. By May 2005 they had reached 75 per cent ownership, allowing them to de-list the club on the London Stock Exchange. By the end of June, the Glazers had 100 per cent ownership of the club for a total price of around £800m.

Because the Glazers used bank loans to partly fund the purchase, it left Manchester United with a massive £660m debt (and repayments of £62m per year). Fans worried that the club – previously without debt – would be unable to compete in the transfer market, and that results would suffer.

On the pitch, Manchester United has continued to succeed. Off the pitch, the Glazer family has recently restructured their loans and reduced the club's debts. Manchester United is not debt-free yet, but it can still compete in the transfer market for the world's best players and is ranked in the top five teams in the world.

Brains
Behind The Brand

Malcolm Glazer
Owner of Manchester United

Glazer was born in New York in 1928, the son of Lithuanian immigrants. In 1943, he inherited his father's watch business. Within five years, he was investing in property – from shopping malls to nursing homes – through his company, First Allied Corporation. In 1995, he bought American football team – the Tampa Bay Buccaneers – and led them to victory in the Super Bowl in 2003. In the same year, he started to buy shares in Manchester United. He died in 2014.

Business Matters

Mergers and acquisitions

This phrase refers to the aspect of company strategy and finance that deals with the buying, selling and combining of different companies. This strategy can help a company grow rapidly within its market by purchasing a separate but complimentary company. An acquisition is the purchase of one company by another company. A merger is when two companies combine to form a third, new company.

Behind the scenes at Manchester United

There's more to a football club than its players. Each club, particularly one as large as Manchester United, has a team of dedicated professionals working behind the scenes to ensure the success of the business.

Manchester United has over 570 permanent employees, mainly based at Old Trafford, the London office, or the training ground at Carrington. Most employees work in one of three areas of business:

Football direct

Largly based at Carrington, and includes the manager, his coaching staff, plus the professional and academy players. It also includes the medical team, sports science, and academy management and welfare. Other personnel at Carrington are the club secretarial department, who manage the fixture lists, as well as travel and accommodation arrangements for home, away and European games.

Commercial

Based at the stadium and includes marketing, sponsorship sales, MU Finance (credit cards), MU Mobile, MU Website, MU Interactive and MUTV (the club's own subscription TV channel). There are other revenue-generating departments, including the ticketing and club membership departments, catering, museums and club tours, and the sales department responsible for the sale of executive private boxes and hospitality packages on a game-by-game or per-season basis. Catering staff regularly feed over 5,000 seated dinner guests on a match day!

Manchester United ground staff prepare the Old Trafford pitch before a game against West Bromwich Albion in December 2012.

Business Matters

Corporate services
The sort of areas you find in all large business, such as finance, HR, legal, IT and communications.

Like many organizations, new recruits are given an induction to make them feel part of the 'family', and to make sure they understand a few key things:
- How employees behave, based on the 'UNITED' values (see box)
- How they are rewarded; pay and benefits
- How they are appraised and how they can improve their performance.

Fortunate newcomers to Manchester United are also taken on a tour of the stadium to visit the museum and trophy room, inspect the changing rooms and sit in the dugout to experience the manager's view of the pitch.

Manchester United kitman Albert Morgan has been at Old Trafford since 1996, and once featured in a Nike ad alongside Cristiano Ronaldo.

Public relations (PR)

Public relations is the practice of conveying messages about the company to the public through the media. The aim is to influence the public's opinion of the company — for example, to view Manchester United not just as a football club, but also as a news delivery service through its mobile and website services. All companies can benefit from positive PR, but it is especially important for football clubs. The goodwill of supporters — especially when a club isn't winning — helps sell match tickets.

The 'UNITED' Values

United with our fans in our commitment and passion for the club

Non-discriminatory in making Manchester United accessible to all, irrespective of age, race, gender, creed or physical ability

Innovative in our ambition to be 'first to the ball' at all times

Team-orientated in our desire to work together with the same dedication displayed in every game by our first team squad

Excelling in our aim to be world class in everything we do

Determined in our pursuit of success while being accountable for our actions

Star power

A company is built on the skills of its workers. While most workers remain anonymous, at a football club the players can become household names and are bought and sold for millions of pounds. The players are some of Manchester United's greatest assets.

From George Best and Bobby Charlton to Eric Cantona, Cristiano Ronaldo and Wayne Rooney, Manchester United has counted some of the biggest names in football on its team sheet. They also haven't been afraid to pay record transfer fees, when necessary, to secure those names.

In 1906, the newly promoted Manchester United signed Herbert Burgess, Jimmy Bannister and winger Billy Meredith from rivals Manchester City. It paid off, with United winning immediate promotion, and clinching their first League title in 1908.

Sir Matt Busby's side was built around youthful homegrown talent, but subsequent managers, such as Tommy Docherty, relied on signings to refresh a failing or ageing side.

A statue of European Cup-winning trio George Best, Denis Law and Bobby Charlton.

THE UNITED TRINITY
BEST LAW CHARLTON

Although large transfer fees can affect a club's cash reserves, they can also improve success on the pitch, meaning greater income from other sources – from match-day ticket sales and prize money to an increased share price.

Way back in 1886, Newton Heath signed well-known players such as Welsh international Jack Powell in order to strengthen their team.

French international Eric Cantona joined the club from rivals Leeds United in 1992. He was known as 'King Eric' by his adoring fans.

Not all signings need to break the bank. One of Sir Alex Ferguson's most valuable signings was the £1.2m acquisition of Frenchman Eric Cantona from Leeds United. In contrast, the transfer of midfielder Roy Keane from Nottingham Forest cost £3.75m, which was an English record-breaking fee in 1993, but is cheap by today's standards!

Cristiano Ronaldo cost £12.24m in the summer of 2003. He struck up a prolific partnership with Wayne Rooney who joined from Everton in 2004 for £25.6 million. Ronaldo went on to become the world's most expensive player when Real Madrid paid £80m for him in 2009.

Football clubs rarely break even on transfers. The net spend of most Premier League clubs per season (the money spent on transfers minus the money recouped from selling players) is around £30 million. Some players are sold on at a loss. United's record signing, Ángel Di María, stayed only a year before he was sold in 2015 to Paris Saint Germain for £44 million, a net loss of £15.7 million.

Dutchman Robin van Persie joined the club from Arsenal in 2012 for a fee of £24 million.

Manchester United's 10 most expensive signings

1 **Angel Di Maria** £59.7m in 2014
2 **Juan Mata** £37.1m in 2014
3 **Anthony Martial** £36m in 2015
4 **Dimitar Berbatov** £30.7m in 2008
5 **Eric Bailly** £30m in 2016
6 **Rio Ferdinand** £29.3m in 2002
7 **Ander Herrera** £29m in 2014
8 **Juan Sebastián Verón** £28.1m in 2001
9 **Marouane Fellaini** £27.5m in 2013
10 **Luke Shaw** £27m in 2014

A global brand

Football has become a global industry, and Manchester United has taken advantage of this growth to expand their fan base around the world.

In 2012, it was reported that Manchester United had doubled their global fan base over five years to a staggering 659 million fans – that's almost 10 per cent of the world's population!

A survey commissioned by the club in 2012 questioned 54,000 people in 39 countries and discovered a global following of 1.6 billion people for the sport, with nearly half naming Manchester United as their favourite team.

According to Manchester United's commercial director, Richard Arnold, the club has twice as many fans in Asia as its closest challenger Barcelona. This support doesn't happen by accident. The club has worked hard to reach a global audience and regularly undertakes promotional tours in countries such as China, Malaysia, South Korea, Sweden, Nigeria, South Africa and the United States.

Manchester United's worldwide appeal dates back to the 1950s, when people were drawn to stories of the Busby Babes. According to European Cup-winner Bobby Charlton, 'Before Munich it was just Manchester's club, but afterwards everyone owned a little bit of it.'

Manchester United players warm up before a friendly in Bangkok, Thailand, during a summer tour in 2013.

Manchester United fans in Kuala Lumpur, Malaysia, enjoy a game against their national side.

The success of Alex Ferguson's side on the pitch undoubtedly aided its commercial growth. At the start of the 1992–93 season, Manchester United's revenue was £25m. By the end of the 2014–15 season – 13 league titles and two Champions Leagues later – it had grown to £395m!

Ferguson's years of success also coincided with a wider growth in English football, with a massive investment in stadiums and players funded by domestic and international TV deals. Manchester United are now estimated to generate the third largest income in world football with £367m, behind Spanish giants Barcelona (£451m) and Real Madrid (£480m).

The club now has a large range of sponsors from noodles to telecommunications companies and strives to maximise off pitch income by forging new partnerships. This can be seen from the playing kit deal struck with Adidas for the 2015–16 season onwards worth as much as £750m over the following ten years and allowing Adidas the exclusive rights to distribute Manchester United sportswear.

Business Matters

Diversification

Companies often decide to offer new products or services — like Manchester United expanding into mobile phones and finance — because it reduces the risk of its other products becoming too limited or uninteresting. By adding new products to its range, the club is providing more reasons for customers to keep returning to the brand.

Brains

Behind The Brand

Richard Arnold
Group Managing Director of Manchester United

Arnold is responsible for the management and growth of the club's sponsorship business, retail, merchandising, clothing and product licensing, plus new media and mobile business. Before joining Manchester United, Arnold worked in international sales and marketing for management consultants InterVoice Ltd where he was twice nominated for Young Director of the Year. He holds a degree in biology from Bristol University.

What does the future hold?

Despite finishing out of the top three for three seasons, Manchester United remains a financial powerhouse with projected revenues for 2016 set to exceed £500m. Where will future revenue growth come from?

There are four main areas that the club is focusing on for future growth:

Increase sponsors
A football club with global awareness can attract global sponsors. Manchester United mix local sponsors in countries from Laos to Bulgaria, with global brands like Chevrolet and DHL. The club now has offices in Asia and North America to make the recruitment of new sponsors easier.

Sell more products to more people
The club plans to expand its range of branded products, as well as improving worldwide distribution, and updating e-commerce channels. Manchester United stores have opened in Singapore, Macau, India and Thailand, with more planned over the next few years.

Manchester United's commercial department has official sponsors of everything from travel, to wine, paint and outdoor clothing.

Selected global partners

Yanmar official diesel engine partner

Aeroflot official carrier

Epson official office equipment supplier

Singha official beer

Casillero del Diablo official wine partner

DHL official logistics partner

Chevrolet official automotive partner

Kansai Paint official paint partner

20th Century Fox official feature film partner

Marathonbet official global betting partner

Columbia official outdoor apparel partner

Business Matters

Long-term success

Successful companies are market-driven, in other words they focus on satisfying the exact section of the market in which they operate. Successful companies also need to be sustainable, which means that the success of the company doesn't just rely on people making use of a company's products and services now, but that they will continue to want to use them in the future.

New media and mobile

Mobile sites, apps and social media are expected to become a much more important way of interacting with – and selling to – the club's global fan base.

Broadcasting revenues

In 2015, Sky and BT signed a three year deal worth £5.14 billion to broadcast Premier League matches from 2016–17. Manchester United made £107.7m from TV and other broadcasting rights to their matches during the 2014–15 season. This figure will rise in the 2016–17 season and is likely to help push the club past £500m in revenue per year.

Former manager Sir Alex Ferguson attend a Chevrolet-sponsored event in Shanghai, China in July 2012.

Design your own merchandise!

To create a new product, for example a new piece of Manchester United merchandise, it is helpful to write a product development brief like the one below. This sample brief is for a new SmartWatch called Fergie Time.

The SWOT analysis on the page opposite will help you to think about the strengths, weaknesses, opportunities and threats for your product. This can help you to see how feasible and practical your idea is before you think of investing time and money in it.

Product Development Brief

Name of product: Fergie Time

Type of product: This is a SmartWatch that, when linked via Bluetooth to your smartphone and an MUTV subscription, will give you news, live text commentary and video highlights of all your team's matches, home and away, in the UK and Europe.

The product explained (use 25 words or less):
Every tackle, every goal, every heart-stopping moment. All there on your wrist! Fergie Time is the ultimate way to follow the world's favourite team.

Target age of users: All ages can use this product.

What does the product do?: Fergie Time allows you to follow every kick of every Manchester United game, as well as up-to-the-minute team news – all on your wrist.

Are there any similar products already available?:
There are several SmartWatches on the market, but none with a team affiliation.

What makes your product different?: We believe that Fergie Time will appeal to Manchester United fans around the world for its great access to team news and exclusive content.

SWOT Analysis
(Strengths, Weaknesses, Opportunities and Threats)

Name of product you are assessing...
Fergie Time

The table below will help you assess your product. By addressing all four areas, you can make your product stronger and more likely to be a success.

Questions to consider

Does your product offer something unique?

Is there anything innovative about it?

What are its USPs (unique selling points)?

Why will people use this product instead of a similar one?

Strengths

There are no other products currently available offering the same service.

Fergie Time's USP is that it's the only product to offer the innovation of a SmartWatch with access to exclusive MUTV services.

Why wouldn't people use this product?

Can everyone use it?

Does it do everything it says it can?

Weaknesses

Fergie Time is a niche service, in that it appeals solely to Manchester United fans. Fans of other football clubs will not buy it.

Users have to be over 16 to subscribe to the MUTV SmartWatch, or have parents' permission.

A SmartWatch will only work where there is a mobile phone signal. We believe it has 95 per cent mobile coverage in the UK. Other parts of the world may vary.

Will the area that the product serves become more important over time?

Can the brand be improved in the future, e.g. adapted for other uses?

Can it be used globally?

Can it develop new USPs?

Opportunities

Smartphone and SmartWatch technology will keep improving, therefore we believe there will be many opportunities to upsell additional updates to the service for existing users, and attract newcomers to the service.

We may also be able to add Smart Glasses to view Fergie Time content in the coming months.

The service can be used around the world, with specially created and targeted content for individual markets.

Is the market that you are selling into shrinking?

Will it face competition from other products?

Are any of your weaknesses so bad they might affect the product in the long run?

Threats

The popularity of Manchester United worldwide is increasing. For continued growth, the team will need to remain high-profile.

Other SmartWatches will appear on the market, but we can exclude them from accessing MUTV content.

Do you have what it takes to work at Manchester United?
Try this quiz!

1) Do you like football?

a) Not really. I sometimes play FIFA 16 on Xbox, but tend to stick to the driving games!

b) I play at school – because we have to – but not in my own time.

c) Yes, love it. I'm in the second XI at school, plus I play for my local side at the weekend.

2) Do you support Manchester United?

a) Nope. I know they wear red shirts, though. Does that help?

b) Everyone in my family is a Chelsea fan – and proud of it!

c) I certainly am. I watch the games when I can, and catch up on team news and gossip online.

3) Who's your favourite Manchester United player?

a) Does Lionel Messi play for them? I always pick him on FIFA.

b) As a Chelsea fan, I don't like any of them, really, but I'd like to have Wayne Rooney in our team.

c) It would have to be Ryan Giggs. Most decorated player in United's history and an inspiration to all the youngsters at the club.

4) What do you want to do when you leave school?

a) Ooh, I haven't thought about that yet. Just hoping to get through my exams first.

b) I want to go to catering college and get a job in a restaurant.

c) I'd love to combine my passions of sport and business – they're both very exciting, fast-moving worlds.

5) If you worked at a football club, what would be your ideal job?

a) Do they have video games tester on the list?

b) Mmm, probably in the kitchens.

c) Wow, I'd love to work in the commercial department. My particular passion would be social media, and extending the club's reach internationally.

6) If you could improve one thing about Manchester United, what would it be?

a) They should stop winning, and give other clubs a chance. Not sure if they would see that as an improvement, though!

b) I don't want to improve them – then Chelsea will never beat them!

c) I think they should look at the emerging markets, and make sure they are offering the growing ranks of fans full access via TV or online to Manchester United games, team news, information and so on.

Results

Mostly As: Sorry, but your chances of working at Manchester United are looking shaky! It doesn't sound like you have the interest or the motivation to succeed in such a high-pressure environment.

Mostly Bs: You are definitely interested in football, but you need to work on your entrepreneurial skills to succeed in a very competitive business.

Mostly Cs: It definitely sounds like you have what it takes to get a job at Manchester United! Keep working hard at school, and keep up your interest and knowledge of the club, and who knows?

Glossary

anonymous someone whose name is not known or made public

astute clever and quick to see how to take advantage of a situation

consecutive following one after another without interruption

consortium: a group of businesses that have joined together to work on a particular project

cumulative including all the amounts that have been added before

de-list to stop a company's shares being traded on a stock market

eclipse to make another person or thing seem much less important

e-commerce the business of buying and selling goods on the Internet

honorary a position for which no payment is received

in its infancy to be very new, still developing

lease a legal agreement to pay money in order to use land or a building, for example, for an agreed period of time

licensee a person who has official permission to do something, in this case sell Manchester United-branded merchandise or services

lucrative producing a lot of money

replica shirt a copy of the official team shirt, worn by fans

surpass to do or be better than someone or something

turmoil a state of confusion or uncertainty

unearth to discover something through careful searching

unprecedented never having happened or existed in the past

winding-up order an order to stop trading or operating

Index